DIY Bath Bombs

made easy

40 Organic DIY Bath Bomb Recipes
for Fragrant Skin And A Rejuvenating
Bath Experience

DISCLAIMER

Introduction

Homemade bath bombs are a super-fun initiative erupting throughout DIY-enthusiast communities everywhere—those of us who wish to feel good, smell good, and de-stress without breaking the bank. Bath bombs are incredible because you can make them all at once, store them for many months at a time, and even buy many ingredients in bulk for added saving bonuses. Think about it, after one afternoon of bath bomb creation, you can have six months of beautiful baths—for very, very cheap.

As you create your own bath bombs, you take charge—or become "the bomb" of your own shopping excursion, in that you disallow yourself to spend a great deal of money on commercial bath products. Plus, you can pass on your passion of DIY by gifting these babies out to people for baby showers, bridal showers, regular group showers (if applicable), and even make them for profit.

In this book, find fresh and zesty bath bombs, sensational bath bombs (that speak to the softer side of skin care), milky bath bombs for a titillating experience, seasonal bath bombs for the seasonal enthusiasts among us (looking at you Miss I-Love-Autumn), and earthy bath bombs. No matter your favorite flavor, your current mood, or the present state-of-the-world, there's a bath bomb in this book for you. Especially given that baths are one of the number-one recommended activities for super-stressed people.

Remember that store-bought make up and beauty products are pulsing with additives that ultimately put you at-risk of serious disorders. Remember that when you place toxins on your skin, these toxins are taken into your body and ultimately into your cells—boosting signs of aging, among so many other unattractive bodily things. However when you utilize real, stunning, natural ingredients for your bath time excursions, you're doing more than working to de-stress yourself. You're further naturalizing your environment and giving yourself hope for a healthy future.

Table of Contents

Chapter 3: Smooth and Silky, Milky

Chapter 4: Floral Bath Bombs 53

Chapter 5: Earthy, Spicy

Bath Bomb "Before You Start" Shopping List

If you're ready to make at-home bath bombs, you should have the following equipment:

Baking Soda: Fine food grade Sodium Bicarbonate is best. Technical grade may contain unwanted impurities, and granular varieties will result in a coarse-looking bath bomb.

Cornstarch: Cornstarch helps control the fizzing reaction between the ingredients as you are mixing.

Citric Acid: Which you can get this from wine making suppliers, some supermarkets, spice shops, or online. Super-fine granules (table salt-sized) are best. Powder is too volatile, whilst coarse granules have a lumpy appearance and may "bobble" as your bath bombs dry out.

Essential Oils: Can be found in small amounts at places like health food stores and craft stores and online.

Spritzer bottle

Witch Hazel: Some people find it easier to use witch hazel in their spritzer bottle over water. Water has a tendency to "set off" the bath bomb's active ingredients before the intended time, hence the witch hazel. However, water works just fine if you keep mixing it in. Witch hazel also speeds the drying time of your bath bombs, allowing you to remove them from their molds faster. If you don't mind the extra expense, you may find it's worth it. For the purposes of this book, witch hazel and water can be used interchangeably. As in all things, use your own discretion and common sense!

Rubber gloves: Citric acid is a skin irritant; always use gloves when handling and mixing.

Plastic or glass mixing bowl.

Mold of your choice: Many of the recipes contained herein have suggestions for molds, but use what you have available and follow your heart!

A Note About Bath Bomb Storage

Remember that you should store them only after the bath bombs are completely dry; otherwise, they'll crumble away into nothing.

Furthermore, you should utilize an airtight container (like Tupperware). This is because high humidity and moisture activate bath bombs.

Always make sure to store flavors/scents separately, as scents can combine/meld together over time.

Always use each bath bomb within six months. After all: oil and water are present in most of the recipes; quality will degrade after 6 months. No preservatives are used, hence the shelf life (and the safety upon your skin!).

Chapter 1:

FRESH AND ZESTY
BATH BOMB RECIPES

Mandarin Sweet Orange Bath Bombs

Ingredients:

1 cup baking soda
3/4 cup cornstarch
1/2 cup powdered citric acid
2 tsp. mandarin essential oil
Red and yellow food coloring (Optional)

Directions:

Combine and mix up the baking soda, cornstarch, and powdered citric acid in a bowl.

Slowly and carefully add in the mandarin essential oil. Pause frequently to stir. At this time, you can optionally add red and yellow drops of food coloring at a ratio of two drops of yellow for every one drop of red to the mixture. Stir well to bring the entire mixture to a pleasing mandarin orange color.

Press the orange mixture firmly into the molds of your choice. If the mixture gets too dry, moisten it with a spritz or two from the witch hazel or water bottle. Let the mandarin bath bombs dry completely overnight.

Remove them gently from the molds once dry. Move the bath bombs immediately to storage in an airtight container, away from moisture.

Enjoy at your leisure!

Twisted Lemon and Lime Bath Bombs

Ingredients:

3/4 cup cornstarch
1 cup baking soda
1/2 cup powdered citric acid
1 tsp. almond oil
1 tsp. lemon essential oil
1 tsp. lime essential oil
Yellow and green food coloring
Plastic, clear snap-together molds

Directions:

Bring together all the dry ingredients—the cornstarch, baking soda, and citric acid—in a mixing bowl. Stir well.

Carefully add in the almond oil and stir. When it is fully mixed in, begin to slowly pour in the essential oils while stirring.

Separate the mixture into two halves and place each half in its own bowl. Add yellow drops of food coloring to one bowl and green drops of food coloring to the other. Stir each bowl well to fully mix in the dye.

With each snap-together mold, press the green mixture firmly into one half and the yellow mixture into the other half. Then snap the mold together. This should result in a final bath bomb that is half-green on one hemisphere and half-yellow on the other.

Don't be afraid to use a few sprays of the spritzer with water or witch hazel to re-moisten the mixture as you are fitting it into the molds.

Give the lemon-lime bath bombs plenty of time to completely dry. This process can take up to 48 hours.

Check for dryness with your hand, then pull them from the molds and store them in an airtight container until they are ready to be used. Enjoy with a margarita!

Fresh Lemon Bath Bombs

Ingredients:

1 cup baking soda
1/2 cup powdered citric acid
3/4 cup cornstarch
1 1/2 tsp. lemon eucalyptus essential oil
1 tsp. spearmint essential oil

Directions:

Put dry ingredients in a bowl and mix well so that there are no clumps. This includes the baking soda, citric acid, and cornstarch.

Patiently pour the essential oils into the mix, pausing often to stir them in.

Give the mixture one to three spritzes of witch hazel or water. Stir well to prevent the ingredients from reacting. When the mixture is of the same consistency as wet sand, pack it firmly into molds of your choice.

Let the lemon bombs dry completely. I like to leave the out overnight in a cool place.

Remove from the molds carefully when dry. Store your new lemony bath bombs in an airtight container until you're ready to use them.

Bittersweet Grapefruit Bath Bombs

Ingredients:

1/2 cup powdered citric acid
3/4 cup cornstarch
1 cup baking soda
2 tsp. grapefruit essential oil
Red and yellow food coloring (Optional)

Directions:

Combine in a mixing bowl all of the dry ingredients—citric acid, cornstarch, and baking soda.

Carefully pour in the essential oil while stirring constantly.

Optionally at this point, you may add in red and yellow drops of food coloring and stir to change the mixture to orange. The best ratio to achieve a "grapefruit-like" color is three drops of red food coloring to every two yellow.

Give the final mixture a few sprays of the witch hazel of water spritzer to make it workable, like wet sand. Press this mixture into the molds you picked out. Use a firm, steady hand.

Leave the molds out to dry completely. Wait 48-72 hours. Check by touch to be sure they are dry, then remove the fresh bath bombs gingerly from the molds and place them in an airtight container until you are ready to use them.

"Dreamsicle" Bath Bombs

Ingredients:

1 cup baking soda
3/4 cup cornstarch
1/2 cup powdered citric acid
1 tsp. vanilla essential oil
1 tsp. sweet orange essential oil
Red and yellow food coloring (Optional)

Directions:

Take all the dry ingredients (baking soda, cornstarch, and citric acid), and bring them together in a mixing bowl. Stir until they are of a uniform consistency.

Pour the essential oils into the bowl slowly, stirring all the while.

Optionally, add just a few alternating drops of food coloring. To achieve the perfect "dreamsicle" color, add only one drop of red food color to every three yellow. Stir well to evenly distribute all the dye.

Pack the resulting mixture into your chosen molds. If the mixture is dry, crumbly, or uncooperative, spritz it a few times with water or witch hazel.

Leave the molds out to dry in a cool place. Check on them after four hours. If dry to the touch, transfer them gently to an airtight container.

Use within sixth months and enjoy!

"Nutty" Orange Bath Bombs

Ingredients:

1 cup baking soda
3/4 cup cornstarch
1/2 cup powdered citric acid
1 tsp. nutmeg essential oil
1 tsp. cardamom essential oil
1 tsp. bitter orange essential oil
Red, yellow, and green food coloring
(Optional)

Directions:

Mix together all the dry ingredients in a glass or plastic bowl. Those ingredients are the baking soda, cornstarch, and citric acid.

Slowly add in the essential oils, one spoonful at a time. Stir well after every spoonful.

At this point, you may optionally pour in alternating drops of the red and yellow food coloring. Stir to make an orange mixture. Then, optionally, add a drop or two of green food coloring and stir to turn the mixture a nutty brown and orange.

If the mixture is dry, spray a few times with water or witch hazel. Then, pack the mixture firmly into the selected molds.

Let the mixture completely dry in the molds before you remove the finished bath bombs and place them in an airtight container of your choosing.

Chapter 2:

SENSATIONAL
SKIN-TASTIC
BATH BOMBS

Cleansing Tea Tree Bath Bombs

Ingredients:

1/4 cup baking soda

1/2 cup cornstarch

1/4 cup powdered citric acid

3 tbsp. almond oil

3 tbsp. coconut oil

1/4 cup shea butter

2 tsp. tea tree essential oil

Directions:

Mix together all the dry ingredients in a plastic or glass bowl. Be sure it's of an even consistency. Fold and work in the coconut oil and shea butter next.

Slowly and carefully add in the almond oil and tea tree oil. Stir frequently to prevent unnecessary fizzing.

Press the resulting mixture into molds of your choosing. If the mixture dries out or misbehaves, spray it once or twice with the water or witch hazel spritzer. The mixture should take shape in your hands and keep it.

Leave the molds out to dry completely. Give them adequate time; I like to leave them out overnight and check again in the morning.

Remove your new bath bombs and store them post haste in an airtight container, away from all moisture. Use when you are ready and enjoy!

White Tea Bath Bombs

Ingredients:

1/2 cup citric acid
1 cup baking soda
1/2 cup cornstarch
2 tbsp. Epsom salt
2 tbsp. coconut oil
2 tbsp. strong white tea of your choosing
1 tsp. essential oil of your choosing (optional)—for this recipe, I use either lemon, lavender, or germanium oils

Directions:

Make your white tea and wait for it to cool.

Mix together the dry ingredients (baking soda, citric acid, cornstarch, and Epsom salt) in a bowl, making sure there are no clumps.

Add in the coconut oil to the mixture, working it in thoroughly. I use a whisk for this step.

Slowly add in the white tea and optional essential oil one spoonful at a time, mixing after each time.

Press the resultant mixture into your molds generously, the pack it down.
Wait for the bath bombs to dry completely, and then gently remove them from the molds.

Store in an airtight container away from moisture until you are ready to use your new bath bombs. Enjoy your restorative bath.

Relaxing Roman Chamomile Bath Bombs

Ingredients:

1/2 cup cornstarch
1/4 cup baking soda
1/4 cup powdered citric acid
1/4 cup shea butter
3 tbsp. coconut oil
3 tbsp. almond oil
2 tsp. roman chamomile essential oil

Directions:

Combine together all the dry ingredients in a bowl—cornstarch, baking soda, and citric acid. Work out any clumps.

Fold in and stir the shea butter next. Then work in the coconut oil.

Slowly and carefully add in the two oils. Stir frequently to prevent unnecessary fizzing.

Pack the mixture into your molds. Spray it with the witch hazel or water spritzer if necessary; this can help it stay moist and keep its shape.

Allow the bath bombs plenty of time to dry in the molds. This process can take up to 48 hours.

Remove gingerly and store in an airtight container when you have made sure they are completely dry.

Immortality Bath Bombs

Ingredients:

1/2 cup cornstarch
1/4 cup powdered citric acid
1/4 cup baking soda
1/4 cup shea butter
3 tbsp. coconut oil
3 tbsp. almond oil
2 tsp. carrot seed essential oil

Directions:

Bring together the cornstarch, citric acid, and baking soda in a bowl. Stir well. Add the shea butter and coconut oil next. Work it in fully with your hands.

One teaspoon at a time, pour in the almond oil and carrot seed oil. Stir after every spoonful.

Press this final mixture into the molds of your choosing.

If the mixture becomes dry as you are working with it, give it a couple sprays of the old water or witch hazel spritzer and stir to whip it back into shape.

Give the bath bombs plenty of time to dry in the molds. Bath bombs tend to crumble if you remove them from their molds before they have dried completely. Store in an airtight container once you have successfully pried them all free.

Rejuvenating, Fresh Bath Bombs

Ingredients:

1/4 cup baking soda
1/4 cup powdered citric acid
1/2 cup cornstarch
1/4 cup Shea butter
3 tbsp. coconut oil
3 tbsp. almond oil
1 1/2 tsp. geranium essential oil
1 1/2 tsp. lemon essential oil

Directions:

Combine the dry ingredients in a mixing bowl. Stir together completely.

Add in the Shea butter and coconut oil, one after the other. Fold them in so they fully become part of the mixture.

Gently pour in the essential oils and the almond oil a bit at a time. Pause frequently to stir.

Push the resulting mixture into the molds you picked out. Use a firm hand. Don't be afraid to overfill the molds generously and then scrape the excess.

Leave the bath bombs in their molds to completely dry. When this has occurred, pop them out of the molds and transfer them straightaway to an airtight container, where they will reside until you are ready to use them. Enjoy your fizzy bath!

Tahitian Cream Bath Bombs

Ingredients:

1/2 cup cornstarch
1/4 cup baking soda
1/4 cup citric acid
3 tbsp. almond oil
3 tbsp. coconut oil
1/4 cup Shea butter
1 tsp. monoi essential oil
1 tsp. vanilla essential oil

Directions:

Bring together the baking soda, citric acid, and cornstarch in a bowl. Mix together fully.

Add in the Shea butter and coconut oil, one after the other. Fold them in so they fully become part of the mixture. Then pour in the almond oil and mix well.

Pour in the essential oils slowly, stirring continuously.

Pack the mixture firmly into your chosen molds. If the mixture dries out as you are working with it, spray it once or twice with water or witch hazel.

Let the bath bombs completely dry. This can take up to 48 hours.

When the bath bombs are completely dry to the touch, remove them and place them in an airtight container.

Chapter 3:

SMOOTH AND SILKY, MILKY BATH BOMBS

Silky Lavender Bath Bombs

Ingredients:

1 cup baking soda
1 cup powdered citric acid
1/2 cup cornstarch
1/4 cup Epsom salt
1/4 cup powdered milk
2 tbsp. softened cocoa butter
2 tbsp. almond oil
2 tsp. lavender essential oil
Blue and red food coloring (Optional)

Directions:

Combine the dry ingredients in a glass or plastic mixing bowl. Stir well.
Add the cocoa butter next. Fold it in so it is part of the mixture.

Slowly pour in the almond oil and essential oils at this point, a bit at a time. Pause frequently to stir.

Optionally here, pour in alternating drops of the blue and red food coloring and stir to achieve a pleasant purple tone.

If the mixture is dries out on you, spray it a few times with water or witch hazel.
Press the mixture firmly into your molds.

Let the mixture completely dry. This can take up to two days. When they are completely dry to the touch, remove them from the molds and place them in an airtight container, away from moisture. Enjoy a relaxing evening!

Land of Milk and Honey Bath Bombs

Ingredients:

1 cup baking soda
1/2 cup cornstarch
1 cup powdered citric acid
1/2 cup powdered milk
2 tbsp. softened cocoa butter
2 tbsp. olive oil
1 tsp. beeswax essential oil

Directions:

In a bowl, mix together the dry ingredients. This includes the baking soda, cornstarch, powdered milk, and citric acid. Use a whisk if you find it necessary.
Pour in the cocoa butter and olive oil while stirring.

Continuing to stir, add in the beeswax essential oil a little bit at a time. Spritz with your bottle of water or witch hazel to moisten the mix into a workable substance. Take this step slowly, checking after each spray.

Press the mixture firmly into the molds of your choice. Remoisten the mixture as you go along, if necessary.

Wait a day and check to see if the bath bombs are dry to the touch. If so, remove them gently from the molds and store away from moisture in an airtight container.

Vanilla Cream Bath Bombs

Ingredients:

1 cup powdered citric acid
1/2 cup cornstarch
1 cup baking soda
1/3 cup Epsom salt
1/4 cup powdered milk
2 tbsp. softened cocoa butter
2 tbsp. olive oil
2 tsp. vanilla essential oil

Directions:

Bring together all of the dry ingredients in a mixing bowl. Stir until uniform. Add in the cocoa butter and stir.

Slowly pour in the oils. Stir continuously during this step.

Pack the resulting mixture in your molds. If, while you are working with it, the mixture begins to dry out, spray it a few times with witch hazel or water and stir thoroughly to work it in.

After the molds are fully packed, leave them to dry overnight. Check in the morning that they are dry to the touch.

Remove safely when dry, store in an airtight container, and enjoy when ready!

Wake Up! Bath Bombs

Ingredients:

1 cup baking soda
1/2 cup cornstarch
1 cup powdered citric acid
1/4 powdered milk
1/4 cup Epsom salt
2 tbsp. softened cocoa butter
2 tbsp. almond oil
2 tsp. coffee essential oil

Directions:

In a glass or plastic mixing bowl, stir together until uniform all of the dry ingredients. This includes the baking soda, cornstarch, powdered milk, Epsom salt, and citric acid.

Add and stir in the cocoa butter until it is well incorporated with the mixture.
Pour in the almond and coffee oil gently. Stir constantly.

Press this mixture firmly into your molds. Overfill the molds, press it in tight, and scrape off the excess mixture. If the mixture dries out on you during this process, spray it once or twice with witch hazel or water and stir.

Provide adequate time for the mixture to dry. This process can take up to two days.

Store safely away from light and moisture in an airtight container until you are ready to use your new Wake Up! Bath bombs. Enjoy!

Chocolate Milk Bath Bombs

Ingredients:

1 cup baking soda
1 cup powdered citric acid
1/2 cup cornstarch
1/2 cup powdered milk
1/4 cup Epsom salt
2 tbsp. softened cocoa butter
2 tbsp. almond oil
2 tsp. chocolate peppermint essential oil

Directions:

Bring together in a bowl all of the dry ingredients—baking soda, citric acid, cornstarch, powdered milk, and Epsom salt.

Fold in the cocoa butter and stir.

With great care, pour in the almond oil and chocolate peppermint oil. Stir continuously.

Spray the mixture once or twice with the water or witch hazel spritzer and stir. Repeat if the mixture dries out on you at any point in the process.

Pack the resulting mixture into your molds of choice, firmly.

Let the mixture dry out in the molds at least overnight. Check by touch to be sure they are completely dry before removing them from their molds. Store immediately in an airtight container.

Chapter 4:

FLORAL
BATH BOMBS

Rose Petal Bath Bombs

Ingredients:

1/4 cup baking soda
1/2 cup cornstarch
1/4 cup powdered citric acid
3/8 cup cocoa butter
3 tbsp. coconut oil
3 tbsp. almond oil
1 tsp. geranium essential oil
1 tsp. rose essential oil
Dried rose petals
Red food coloring (Optional)

Directions:

Combine all dry ingredients in a mixing bowl. This includes the baking soda, cornstarch, and powdered citric acid. Mix them so that the resulting mixture has a fine consistency.

Add and work in the cocoa butter. Then, do the same with the coconut oil. Slowly add the almond and essential oils. Pause frequently to stir the oil in completely.

Place a rose petal or two in the bottom of each of your molds of choice. Press the mixture firmly into the molds. If the mixture is not cooperating, give it some sprays from your water or witch hazel spritzer. I also like to tear a petal up and mix it in with the bath bomb as I pack the mixture into my molds.

Let the rose bath bombs dry completely for a minimum of four hours. Do not remove them too early or they are liable to crumble. When they are dry to the touch, remove your bath bombs and store them in an airtight container away from moisture. Enjoy!

"Purple Rain" Bath Bombs

Ingredients:

1/2 cup cornstarch
1/4 cup baking soda
1/4 cup powdered citric acid
3 tbsp. almond oil
3 tbsp. coconut oil
3/8 cup Shea butter
1 tsp. lavender essential oil
1 tsp. blue chamomile essential oil
Dried lavender or lilac flowers
Red and blue food coloring (Optional)

Directions:

Place in a bowl and mix all the dry ingredients—cornstarch, baking soda, and citric acid, avoiding clumps.

Fold and work in the Shea butter. Then, do the same with the coconut oil.

Pour in the essential oils and almond oil one teaspoon at a time, stirring constantly. Optionally, at this point you may add one drop each of the red and blue food coloring and stir this in to the mixture to give your future bath bombs the slightest purple shade.

Place some dried flowers in the bottom of your molds. This will form a pleasant garnish on top of the bath bombs when finished.

Spray the mixture with water or witch hazel and stir until you can form it into shapes with your hands. Press this mixture into your prepared molds with firm, consistent pressure.

Leave the molds out to dry in a cool place overnight. Check them the next day to be sure they are dry before removing them from their molds.

Place your new lavender bath bombs in a container free from moisture and store until use.

Floral Honey Bath Bombs

Ingredients:

1 cup baking soda
3/4 cup cornstarch
1/2 cup powdered citric acid
1 tsp. neroli essential oil
1 tsp. beeswax essential oil
Yellow food coloring
Bee or honeycomb-themed mold

Directions:

In a bowl, mix together the baking soda, cornstarch, and citric acid. Use a whisk if necessary.

A little bit at a time, add in the essential oils. Stir throughout this process. Add food coloring one drop at a time and stir after until your have reached the shade of yellow your prefer for your bath bombs.

Spritz with your bottle of water or witch hazel to moisten the mix into a workable substance.

Press resulting mixture with consistent firm pressure into molds. I have hexagon-shaped molds I use for this recipe, but use whatever you have at hand. Several websites that sell soap-making supplies have honeycomb or bee hive-shaped molds that look wonderful.

Wait at least four hours for the bath bombs to completely dry. Do not attempt to remove them from their molds until they are dry. Remove your bath bombs and store in an airtight container, away from moisture.

New World Bath Bombs

Ingredients:

1 cup baking soda
1/2 cup powdered citric acid
3/4 cup cornstarch
2 tsp. jasmine essential oil
Dried jasmine flowers or other dried flowers

Directions:

Place the baking soda, citric acid, and cornstarch in a bowl and stir thoroughly. Slowly add in the jasmine oil, stirring as you do so.

Prepare your molds of choice by placing dried flowers in the bottom of each one. This will effectively "garnish" the tops of your bath bombs.

Give the mixture some sprays of witch hazel or water to help it form into clumps. Press this mixture firmly into the prepped molds.

Let the jasmine bath bombs completely dry. This process takes multiple hours.

Later, check for dryness. If they feel ready, carefully remove the bath bombs from the molds and immediately move them into an airtight container away from moisture. Store them there until use and enjoy!

Evergreen Floral Dream Bath Bombs

Ingredients:

1 cup baking soda
1/2 cup cornstarch
1 cup powdered citric acid
1/4 cup Epsom salt
1/4 cup powdered milk
2 tbsp. softened cocoa butter
2 tbsp. olive oil
1 1/2 tsp. ylang ylang essential oil
1/2 tsp. vanilla essential oil
Dried mixed flowers

Directions:

Combine and mix all dry ingredients in a glass bowl. This includes the baking soda, cornstarch, citric acid, Epsom salt, and powdered milk. Stir until it is all of the same consistency.

Add in the cocoa butter and work it until it is of a part with the mixture. After, pour in the olive oil slowly and stir it in completely.

Slowly, while stirring, add in the essential oils. Don't worry too much if the mixture starts to fizz on you; just mix it up vigorously until it ceases. Prep the molds by dropping a few dried flowers in the bottom of each one.

Press the mixture into molds firmly. If the mixture is too dry and crumbly, spray it with the water or witch hazel spritzer once or twice.

Allow these floral bath bombs to dry in a cool place. Remove them from the molds only when they have dried completely and store them immediately in an airtight container of your discretion. For best use, use these amazing bath bombs within six months. Enjoy!

Relaxing Perfumed Bath Bombs

Ingredients:

1/2 cup powdered citric acid
3/4 cup cornstarch
1 cup baking soda
1 tsp. yuzu essential oil
1 tsp. cypress essential oil

Directions:

Combine the citric acid, cornstarch, and baking soda in a mixing bowl. Stir the mixture constantly as you slowly add in the essential oils.

Spray the mixture frugally with your spritzer full of witch hazel of water, stirring after each spray. The mixture will be ready when you can form it into clumps with your hands. Press this mixture steadily into the selected molds. Don't be afraid to overfill the molds then pack them down and scrape off the excess.

Let the bath bombs dry in the molds at least overnight.

Later, after checking for adequate dryness by touch, gently pull the fresh bath bombs from the molds. Store them safely in an airtight, moisture-less container. Use within six months and enjoy!!

Chapter 5:

EARTHY, SPICY BATH BOMBS

"Freshly Mown" Lemongrass Bath Bombs

Ingredients:

1 cup baking soda
3/4 cup cornstarch
1/2 cup powdered citric acid
1 tsp. lemongrass essential oil
1 tsp. cardamom essential oil
Green food coloring

Directions:

Combine and mix all dry ingredients in a glass mixing bowl.

One teaspoon at a time, carefully pour in essential oils and stir thoroughly. It should start to form clumps like wet sand. Add spritzes of water or witch hazel to assist in this.

Add a couple drops of green food coloring and stir it in to give the future bath bombs a nice green tint.

When the mixture is starting to form satisfactory clumps, pack it into your molds firmly and generously. Allow them to dry overnight.

Check to be sure they are completely dry before removing your new bath bombs from the molds. Move immediately to an airtight container and store until you are ready to gift or use.

Bold Balancing Bath Bombs

Ingredients:

3/4 cup cornstarch
1/2 cup powdered citric acid
1 cup baking soda
1 tsp. vetiver essential oil
2 tbsp. almond oil
Red and green food coloring (optional)

Directions:

Pour all the dry ingredients into a mixing bowl and stir. When it is finely mixed, begin to slowly add the oils. Stop to stir frequently.

Optionally, add alternating drops of red and green food coloring and stir until you achieve a pleasant brown color.

Spritz the mixture with your water or witch hazel until you can form it into clumps with your hands.

Press the mixture firmly into your molds of choice. Don't be afraid to overfill it and then pack it down tight.

Allow the mixture to dry out completely someplace cool. The drying process often takes upwards of 48 hours.

Once the bath bombs are completely dry, move and store them in an airtight container, away from moisture. They are best if used within six months.

Bitter Spices Bath Bombs

Ingredients:

1 cup baking soda
1/2 cup powdered citric acid
3/4 cup cornstarch
1 tsp. black pepper essential oil
1 tsp. bitter orange essential oil
Red and yellow food coloring (optional)
Dried herbs or spices—I use sage and
rosemary

Directions:

Note: black pepper oil will not make you
sneeze.

Place the baking soda, citric acid, and
cornstarch in a bowl together and mix
well.
With great care, add the oils a bit at a time
to the mixture. Pause with frequency to
stir. Keeping your proto-bath bombs well
mixed is crucial to preventing them from
fizzing ahead of schedule.

Garnish the bottom of each mold with a pinch of the dried herbs or spices. Then, press the resulting mixture firmly into your selected molds. Give the mixture multiple spritzes of your witch hazel or water to get it to cooperate with the process.

Give the mixture plenty of time to dry in the molds. Removing the bath bombs too early causes them to crumble.

Check for adequate dryness and carefully remove the new bath bombs. Store them safely away in an airtight container.

Incensed Bath Bombs

Ingredients:

1 cup baking soda
1/2 cup powdered citric acid
3/4 cup cornstarch
1/4 cup Epsom salt
3 tbsp. coconut oil
2 tbsp. almond oil
1 tsp. sandalwood essential oil
1 tsp. bay essential oil
Red, green, and yellow food coloring (optional)

Directions:

Combine all dry ingredients (baking soda, citric acid, cornstarch, and Epsom salt) in a bowl. Mix until uniform.

Add and work in the coconut oil.

Slowly add in the oils to the mixture a bit at a time. Optionally, you may add alternating red and green food coloring drops and stir them in for a nice brown color. Add a drop of yellow food coloring to turn it to a lighter brown.

Carefully spritz the mixture a couple times with your water or witch hazel. Work and fold the mixture to avoid it reacting early. When you can form it into clumps with your hands, begin to pack the mixture into your molds. Press firmly to assure it fills out the entire mold.

Let the mixture dry out fully overnight in the molds. Allow for more time if needed. Remove carefully from the molds and store in an airtight, moisture-less container. Bath bombs are best if used within six months. Enjoy your spiritual, relaxing bath!

"Mother Earth" Hippie Bath Bombs

Ingredients:

1 cup baking soda
1/2 cup powdered citric acid
1/2 cup cornstarch
1/4 cup Dead Sea salt
3 tbsp. coconut oil
2 tbsp. almond oil
1 tsp. patchouli essential oil
1 tsp. oakmoss essential oil

Directions:

Combine and mix up all dry ingredients in a glass bowl. This includes the baking soda, powdered citric acid, cornstarch, and Dead Sea salt.

Mix in the coconut oil and work it fully into the mixture.

Slowly and carefully add the almond and essential oils into the mixture. Stop and stir frequently.

Give the mixture a good spritzing of water or witch hazel. Take care not to let the mixture fizz too much by stirring vigorously. When you can form the mixture with your hands and it keeps its shape, press it into the molds you picked out firmly.

Give the mixture some time to completely dry out. I like to leave them overnight in a cool place and check on them the next day.

Check to be sure the bath bombs are dry to the touch. Remove them gently and place them in an airtight container and store until you are ready to use.

Invigorating Ginger Bath Bombs

Ingredients:

1/2 cup cornstarch
1/4 cup powdered citric acid
1/4 cup baking soda
6 tbsp. Shea butter
3 tbsp. coconut oil
3 tbsp. almond oil
1 tsp. ginger essential oil
Red and yellow food coloring (optional)

Directions:

Mix dry ingredients (citric acid, cornstarch, and baking soda) together well in a bowl.

Add the Shea butter and coconut oil to the bowl and work them in until you achieve a uniform consistency.

Slowly add in the almond oil and the ginger essential oil a bit at a time, stirring constantly. After this, if desired add a few drops of yellow food coloring and a drop or two of red food coloring and stir the mixture to reach an orange color.

Take the resulting dough-like mixture and press it firmly into your molds. Don't be afraid to re-moisten the mixture with your spritzer as you go along, so that it doesn't dry out while you are working with the molds.

Leave the molds out to dry at least overnight. Depending on your area's climate, this process can take up to 48 hours.

Remove the bath bombs gently from their molds. Store them safely in an airtight container, away from moisture. Enjoy your bath bombs!

Chapter 6:

SEASONAL
BATH BOMBS

Birthday Cake Bath Bombs

Bath Bomb Ingredients:

1 cup baking soda
1/2 cup powdered citric acid
1/4 cup Epsom salt
1/4 cup cornstarch
2 tbsp. cocoa butter
1 tsp. almond oil
1 tsp. vanilla essential oil
Yellow food coloring
Cupcake or muffin tins
Cupcake liners

Icing Ingredients (Optional):

1 1/2 cup powdered sugar
2 1/2 tbsp. meringue powder
1/4 tsp. cream of tartar
4 tbsp. warm, distilled water
1 tbsp. SLS (optional)
1/2 tsp. essential oil of your choice—for icing, I like chocolate peppermint or vanilla
Piping bags and nozzles

Bath Bomb Directions:

Combine and mix all dry ingredients (citric acid, baking soda, cornstarch, Epsom salt) in a bowl. Work in the cocoa butter.

Slowly add in the essential oils a spoonful at a time. Pause frequently to stir. After, add in a drop or two of yellow food coloring and stir it in.

Fill your cupcake tins with liners and pack the mixture firmly into the cupcake liners. Leave the cake bath bombs in the tin until they are completely dry. This takes at least four hours.

Icing Directions (Optional):

Mix the meringue powder and warm distilled water in a bowl. After, you may add the cream of tartar and optional SLS and stir it in.

Add the powdered sugar to the mixture and blend with an electric whisk for at least five minutes until the mixture is frothy and keeps its shape.

Add in the essential oil you have selected and blend it in.
Working quickly before the icing sets, move it into the piping bags and ice your birthday cake bath bombs! After you have completely icing all of the bath bombs, give them 48 hours to set completely.

Store your birthday cake bath bombs away from moisture and be sure to use them within six months. Enjoy!

Valentine's Day Couples' Bath Bombs

Ingredients:

1 cup baking soda
1/2 cup powdered citric acid
1/4 cup cane sugar
3/4 cup cornstarch
2 tsp. essential oils of you choice—here I recommend ylang ylang or jasmine
Red food coloring or, optionally, dried ground berries such as strawberries, raspberries, and blackberries

Directions:

Mix together all the dry ingredients in a bowl. If you've chosen to include dried ground berries, mix those in at this time.

Slowly add in your chosen essential oil (or oils) while stirring. After, you may stir in a few drops of food coloring if you like.

Spray with your water spritzer a few times until you can make it into clumps with your hands. Don't be afraid to repeat this step if the mixture begins to dry out during step four.

Firmly press the mixture generously into your chosen molds. If you have a heart cookie cutter, that's perfect! Otherwise, I just use a flexible silicon ice cube tray.
Let dry completely, at least overnight.

Store in an airtight container (such as a sealed jar or Tupperware container) away from moisture and direct light.

Use on a special occasion within six months and enjoy your steamy, romantic bath!

Easter Egg Bath Bombs

Ingredients:

1/2 cup cornstarch
1/2 cup Epsom salt
1/2 cup powdered citric acid
3 tbsp. water
6 tbsp. almond oil
4 tsp. essential oil of your choice—for this
theme, I like lavender or juniper berry
Pastel food coloring of your choice
Cosmetic glitter (optional)
Plastic Easter eggs

Directions:

Mix dry ingredients in a bowl. Be sure
there are no lumps.

Mix together the wet ingredients in a
separate bowl. Add in just a few drops of
the pastel food coloring you chose to the
mix and stir.

Slowly combine the dry and wet
ingredients. Wearing rubber gloves, stir

with your hands. If the resulting mixture is too dry, spritz with water until the consistency is such that it clumps together easily.

Press your mix into the plastic Easter egg molds one half at a time and then snap the two sides together. Let dry completely.

Store in an airtight container away from moisture. Use within six months. Enjoy your fizzy Easter-style bath!

Party Favor Bath Bombs

Ingredients:

1 cup baking soda
1/2 cup powdered citric acid
1 and 1/2 tsp. essential oil of your choice—for this theme, I like bergamot
Bold food coloring of your choice
Muffin or mini-muffin tin
Confetti!

Directions:

Mix together your dry ingredients (baking soda, powdered citric acid) in a bowl, making sure there are no dreaded lumps.

Slowly add in the oils while stirring. Then add a few drops of the food coloring after that. Stir some more.

Spritz with your spray bottle until your reach a desirable consistency. The mixture should clump together.

Add small confetti pieces to the bottom of each cup of your muffin tin. Press your bomb mixture firmly into the cups over the confetti.

Wait until completely dry. This can take up to 48 hours. Remove and admire! The confetti should be embedded in the top of your new bath bombs. Store in an airtight container away from moisture.

Distribute to your party guests. Remind them to use them within six months and to, of course, enjoy!

Party Time Disco Bath Bombs

Ingredients:

1 cup baking soda

1/2 cup powdered citric acid

3/4 cup cornstarch

1 tsp. star anise essential oil

1 tsp. cosmetic glitter

2 tsp. edible glitter—I use Wilton brand; they look like tiny, silver stars. It can be found online and in some grocery stores' baking sections.

Blue food coloring (optional)

Plastic, snap-together plain Christmas ornaments

Directions:

Note: Do NOT use craft glitter.

Combine the baking soda, citric acid, and cornstarch in a bowl. Mix well.

Slowly add in the star anise oil while stirring. After, mix in the cosmetic glitter and half of the edible glitter.

Add one drop of blue food coloring and stir it in to give your mixture a very light blue hue.

In the bottom of each of your snap-together ornament halves, add a bit of the remaining edible glitter stars. This ensures they will be on the outside of the finished bath bombs. Then, pack your mixture firmly into the molds. Snap the halves together when you have finished. If the mixture begins to dry out at any point in this process, give it a spritz from your water or witch hazel bottle.

Allow twenty-four hours for the bath bombs to completely dry. Gently remove them when you are sure they are ready and move them immediately to an airtight container. Keep them there until you are ready to use one. Enjoy!

Jack O' Lantern Pumpkin Bombs

Ingredients:

1 cup baking soda
3/4 cup cornstarch
1/4 cup Epsom salt
1/2 cup powdered citric acid
2 tbsp. coconut oil
1 tsp. cinnamon essential oil
1 tsp. ginger essential oil
1/2 tsp. nutmeg essential oil
1/2 tsp. clove essential oil
Red and yellow food coloring
Pumpkin-shaped soap molds or cookie cutters

Directions:

Place baking soda, cornstarch, Epsom salt, and citric acid in a mixing bowl and mix thoroughly.

Work in the coconut oil.

Pour in the essential oils slowly, one spoonful at a time. Stir after every spoonful.

Add three drop of the yellow food coloring and two drops of the red food coloring and stir to make your mixture orange. Add drops of either color to the mixture and stir until you reach your desired shade.

Take the mixture and press firmly into the molds. If the mixture starts to dry out during this process, moisten it with your witch hazel or water spritzer.

Allow your bath bombs to dry overnight in a cool place. After checking to be sure they are dry, carefully remove them from the molds.

Store your pumpkin bombs in an airtight container and be sure to use them within six months. Enjoy!

Winter Wonderland Snowballs

Ingredients:

1/4 cup powdered citric acid
1/2 cup baking soda
1/4 cup cornstarch
1/4 cup Epsom salt
2 1/2 tsp. almond oil
2 tsp. essential oil of your choice—for this recipe, I use a combination of spearmint and either pine or fir needle oil
Blue food coloring

Directions:

Mix together the baking soda, cornstarch, Epsom salt, and citric acid in a bowl. Avoid clumps!

Slowly add in wet ingredients while stirring. Mix completely. Add water or witch hazel as necessary for the desired consistency.

Press the mixture firmly into molds. To make snowballs, I use a snowball maker or an ice cream scoop!

Step away and wait patiently for the snowballs to completely dry. Store in an airtight container, away from moisture and humidity. Throw your snowballs into the bath and enjoy!

Christmastime Bath Bomb

Ingredients:

1 cup baking soda
1/2 cup powdered citric acid
3/4 cup cornstarch
1 tsp. Frankincense essential oil
1 tsp. Myrrh essential oil
Red and green food coloring (optional)
Plastic, snap-together Christmas ornaments

Directions:

Mix dry ingredients (baking soda, citric acid, and cornstarch) in a glass mixing bowl. Slowly add in essential oils. Stop to stir them in frequently.

Separate mixture into two halves and place each half in a bowl of its own. Add a few drops of red food coloring to one bowl and stir until the whole mixture is a pleasant shade of red. Repeat this process with the other bowl and the green food coloring.

Keep the mixtures moist using your water or witch hazel spritzer, but don't overdo it.

For each Christmas ornament mold, press the red mixture firmly into one half and the green mixture into the other half. Then snap the mold together. This should result in an ornament that is half-green on one hemisphere and half-red on the other. Don't be afraid to experiment with other patterns!

Let your Christmastime bath bombs completely dry, overnight at minimum. Carefully remove them from the molds when you are certain they are dry.

Store in an airtight container away from moisture, and enjoy your holiday bath experience!

Candy Cane Bath Bombs

Ingredients:

1 cup baking soda
1/4 cup citric acid
Red food coloring
1 tsp. peppermint essential oil

Directions:

Pour your baking soda and citric acid together in a bowl and mix well. Add in the peppermint oil slowly and stir.

Divide mixture into two separate bowls. Add red food coloring to one and mix thoroughly. Don't be afraid to spritz your mixtures with water or witch hazel so that they achieve their optimal consistency.

Press a thin layer of the uncolored mix into your mold of choice. Then add a layer of the red mix atop. Continue alternating layers until your mold is full. This will produce a striped effect.

Let your bath bombs dry completely before attempting to remove them from their molds. This can take up to two days.

Store in an airtight container away from moisture until you are ready to use one.
Admire your amazing candy cane bath bombs and make sure to use them within six months. Enjoy a seasonal bath time experience!

Seasonal Spiced Bath Bombs

Ingredients:

1 cup baking soda
2/3 cup powdered citric acid
1/2 cup Epsom salt
2 tsp. beetroot powder
1 tbsp. almond oil
3 tsp. essential oils—for this recipe, combine cinnamon, orange, and fir needle oils in the ratio most pleasing to you

Directions:

Place the baking soda, citric acid, Epsom salt, and beetroot powder in a bowl. Mix them together thoroughly.

Next add and stir in the almond oil. After that, stir in the cinnamon, orange, and fir needle essential oils.

The beetroot powder should have given your mixture a red tint and a slight sweet scent. Add more or less to the mixture to achieve your desired shade of red.

Using your spritzer, moisten the mixture until you can form it into consistent clumps with your hands.

Using your hands, press the mixture firmly into your molds. I like to use a domed mold for this recipe.

Let dry overnight. If the bath bombs aren't completely dry in the morning, give them more time before removing them from their molds.

With care, remove from their molds and transfer them to an airtight container away from moisture for storage.

Chinese New Year "Fortune Cookie" Bath Bombs

Ingredients:

1 cup baking soda
1 cup powdered citric acid
1/2 cup cornstarch
1/4 cup Epsom salt
1/4 cup powdered milk
2 tbsp. softened cocoa butter
2 tbsp. almond oil
1 tsp. bergamot essential oil
1 tsp. lavender essential oil
Yellow food coloring
Fortune cookie soap or candle mold
Printed, trimmed, and—optimally—laminated "fortune" paper slips (optional)

Directions:

Note: It's not worth making these themed bath bombs without a fortune cookie mold. They can be found at a number of online soap and candle supply vendors with a quick Internet search. I promise it's worth the extra effort.

Combine dry ingredients—cornstarch, citric acid, baking soda, and powdered milk—in a bowl and mix completely.

In a separate bowl, pour in and mix all wet ingredients except the food coloring. Slowly add the contents of the wet ingredients bowl to the dry ingredients bowl, stopping to stir frequently.

Add yellow food coloring to the mix, stirring after every drop, until the desired hue is reached.

Moisten the mixture with your trusty spritzer filled with witch hazel or water. When you have a workable consistency, press the resulting mixture firmly into your fortune cookie molds. Stop halfway up each mold and insert a paper fortune, if you are using them, and then continue to fill the rest of the mold.

Let your fortune bath bombs dry out completely. This process should be allowed to go on at least overnight. After checking that the bath bombs are dry to the touch, remove them from their molds and place them carefully in an airtight storage container.

Conclusion

DIY Bath Bombs Made Easy offers essential health, natural and rejuvenating oils, and a mentality-boosting fizz to each of these bath bomb recipes. So much of the beauty industry is stocked with preservatives, with anti-health ingredients that ultimately you put yourself at-risk for rapid aging and serious diseases. However, if you look to these Shea butters, essential oils, healthful baking sodas, and other incredible ingredients, you know that you're putting stunning, natural health back into your cells. You know that you're giving yourself a chance to live well.

Live your life with vitality, strength, and environmental, natural ingredients. Dive into a fizzy, comfortable bath-bomb fueled bath, and know that you are taking a step toward both your bodily health and the health of the greater world.

Made in the USA
Middletown, DE
08 June 2016